TANDEM

Communicative Practice Materials for Post-Elementary & Intermediate Students of English

Alan Matthews and Carol Read

Bell & Hyman

Published in 1984 by
BELL & HYMAN LIMITED
Denmark House
37-39 Queen Elizabeth Street
London SE1 2QB

Reprinted 1984, 1985

First published in 1980 by
Evans Brothers Limited

We are grateful to the following for their help in the production
of these materials: Mary Spratt for reading and criticising the draft
activities and Teacher's Notes; Edith Foerster and Teresa Nunes
da Silva for typing the manuscript of the Teacher's Notes.

ISBN 0 7135 2378 6   Students
ISBN 0 237 50677 7   Teachers

Cover design by António Mendes
(Illustrations by Melinda Mourão

Printed in Great Britain by
Thetford Press Limited, Thetford, Norfolk

CONTENTS

	1	2	3	4
Name	John White	Sarah Jones		
Age	15	14		
Country	England	United States		

	1	2	3	4
Name		Andrew Martin		John Grant
Age	47			
Job			Housewife	Actor
Country	U.S.A.	England		Ireland

LOST PROPERTY

	MARTA	ROB	BEN	PATRICK
shape?	round			oblong
colour?		black		black and white
size?	small		big	
other information?		small handle	checked	

Who will claim which suitcase?

	SAM	PAUL	BARBARA
how many?	3		2
shape?		oval	square
colour?		bright orange	
how big?	small		big
made of?	plastic		
other information?		four wheels	

	height	build	hair	eyes	features
NICK REEK		slim	short curly		
ROBBIE FAST	very short			green	scar on his face
ANNIE ADDER	tall		long fair		
LORNA STEELE		thin		brown	wears red stockings
JAKE JAWS	short		short dark		smokes big cigars
CHRIS RIPPER		fat		grey	

Which three people must you meet?

Tell your friend to meet:

David: tall
slim
short dark hair
glasses
wearing: jeans and a sweater
carrying: bag and newspaper

Sheila: short
slim
long dark hair
wearing: dress and a jacket
carrying: handbag

Steve: tall
fat
short fair hair
glasses
wearing: jacket and trousers
carrying: suitcase

Arrange on your diagram:

1 sofa

2 armchairs

1 TV table and TV

1 phone table
and phone

1 fireplace

1 bookcase

2 indoor plants

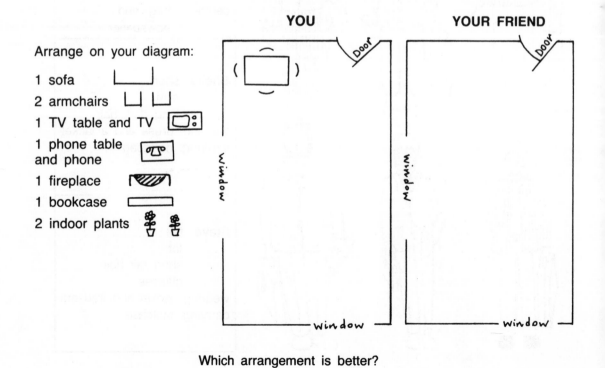

Which arrangement is better?

PAM	having dinner at Steve's house
MIKE	Studying at home
JANE	having dinner with Dan
JENNY	talking to Joy
GEORGE	visiting his girlfriend, Sheila
HARRY	having a drink in the Pub

HELEN	
STEVE	
JOY	
ROBIN	
DAN	
SHEILA	

Who was the murderer?

	GETS UP	BREAKFAST	WORK	LUNCH	DINNER	EVENING
TOM JONES BUS DRIVER	6.00	6.45	7.30 – 4.30	midday in the pub	about 5.00 – after work	meets friends in the pub
JOHN SMITH BANK MANAGER						
SALLY WEST SECRETARY	8.30	9.00	9.30 – 5.30	12.30 in the café	9.00	goes to the cinema and parties
JANE NOLES JOURNALIST						

Time of meeting:

	GETS UP	BREAKFAST	WORK	LUNCH	DINNER	EVENING
JEAN SCOTT LIBRARIAN						
TONY BENSON BANK CLERK						
BILL TAYLOR						
SUE EVANS						

Time of meeting:

	BATH	SYDNEY	NEW ORLEANS	DUNDEE
country?	England		the U.S.A	
which part?	the west			the east coast
population?		3 million		180,000
weather?		hot and dry		windy and cold
what/like?		modern busy	lively commercial	
famous for?	the Roman Baths		Jazz music	

What the TRAVEL AGENT says:

What YOU say:

FLIMTON-ON-SEA
beautiful beaches
hot and dry
quiet
not very expensive
lots to do

TANAWAY
near the lake region
cool and dry
very few tourists
cheap hotels
on bus and train routes

SLACTON
sandy beaches
long hot summer
lots of bars and discos
full of young people
many good hotels

BRECCLES
near the mountains
cold
very quiet
only one restaurant
lovely surroundings

HELTON
sandy beaches outside the town
expensive hotels
beautiful weather
very crowded
nothing to do in the evening

SEAGATE
almost empty beaches
bad, expensive hotels
nowhere good to eat
no tourists or young people
hot, very little rain

Which place will you choose?

Ask your partner how to get to:

a) the Doctor's from Mayfeld   (Write 1 in the box)
b) the Restaurant from Cherston   (Write 2 in the box)
c) the Hairdresser's from Brigg   (Write 3 in the box)

FENLEY-ON-MEAD

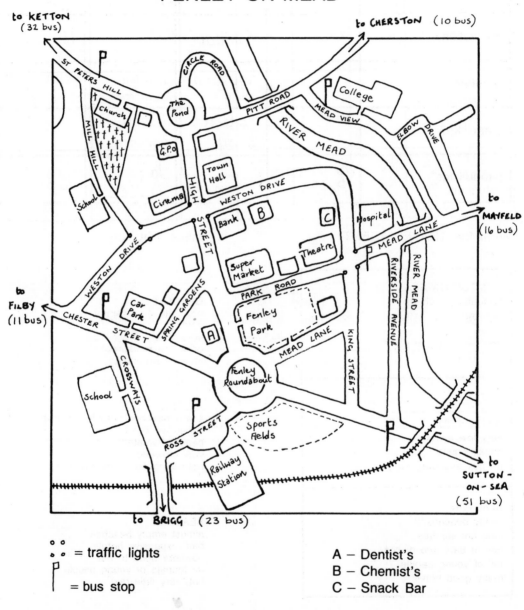

o o
. . = traffic lights

⌐ = bus stop

A – Dentist's
B – Chemist's
C – Snack Bar

Describe your proposed Carnival Route to your partner.
Which is the better route?

THE EARLIEST ROUND-THE-WORLD EXPLORERS

Name	Started journey		Visited		Adventures	Returned home
	Year	Town	Place	Year		
Jean le Monde French	1415	Bordeaux				drowned in India (1417)
John O'World Irish				1421 1424	met cannibals near the Amazon	
Jan Wereld Dutch			India Australia	1431 1433	married an Indian princess	
João Mundo Portuguese	1425	Lisbon		1426 1428		1430

1. Which country is larger?
   a) Portugal   Portugal: 92,000 square kilometres
   b) Ireland

2. Which of these cities has the oldest
   university?
   a) Lisbon   Lima: started in 1551
   b) Lima   Cologne: started in 1388
   c) Cambridge
   d) Cologne

3. Which of these mountains are the
   highest?
   a) The Andes   The Andes: 7000 metres
   b) The Rocky Mountains
   c) The Atlas Mountains

4. Which river is longer?
   a) The Amazon   The Amazon: 6000 kilometres
   b) The Nile

5. Which of these countries has the
   largest population?
   a) France   France: 52 million
   b) Spain   West Germany: 62 million
   c) West Germany
   d) England

6. Which city is further from London?
   a) Lisbon   Rome: 1450 kilometres
   b) Rome

7. Which ocean is the biggest?
   a) The Atlantic   The Pacific: 180 million square kilometres
   b) The Pacific
   c) The Indian

8. Which of these U.S. cities is the
   largest?
   a) Chicago   San Francisco: 720,000
   b) Los Angeles
   c) San Francisco

9. Which town is hotter in summer?
   a) Madrid   Athens: 27°C
   b) Athens

10. Which planet is bigger?
    a) The Earth   The Moon: diameter of 3400 kilometres
    b) The Moon

SKIMPY SNACK BAR	THE CORNER CAFE
Drinks:	**Drinks:**
Glass of milk . . . . 15 p	Pepsi-Cola . . . .
Coca-Cola . . . . 18 p	Lemonade . . . .
Orangeade . . . . 17 p	Cup of white coffee . . . .
Cup of black coffee . . . . 20 p	Cup of black coffee . . . .
Cup of white coffee . . . . 25 p	Cup of tea (with milk) . . . .
Cup of tea (with milk) . . . . 15 p	Cup of tea (with lemon) . . . .
	Glass of milk . . . .
Sandwiches:	
Cheese and tomato . . . . 30 p	**Sandwiches:**
Cheese . . . . 25 p	Ham . . . .
Ham . . . . 28 p	Cheese and tomato . . . .
Ham and cheese . . . . 35 p	Cheese . . . .
Apple tart . . . . 25 p	Lemon pie . . . .
Lemon pie . . . . 20 p	Chocolate cake . . . .

Which cafe is cheaper?

FROM LONDON TO:	BY BUS	BY TRAIN	BY PLANE
MADRID	22 hours	20 hours	£106
PARIS	£13-50	£24-50	35 minutes
ROME		28 hours	£114
ATHENS	40 hours	36 hours	£145
LISBON	£35	£50	2 hours
BONN	12 hours £17-50	11 hours	£75

LONDON TO LISBON	TRAIN I	TRAIN II	TRAIN III
leave from? time?	Victoria station	Victoria station 23.45 Wednesday	
English Channel? how long?	2½ hours	by hovercraft 40 minutes	
arrive/ Paris? leave/Paris?	01.15 Tuesday	7.05 Thursday 10.35 Thursday	
route? arrive/Lisbon?	Toulouse	Bordeaux 8.20 Friday	
price: 1st class? price: 2nd class?	£52-50	£65.00 £45.00	
restaurant car?	Yes	after Paris	
bar?		Yes	
couchettes?		Yes	

Which train will you and your friend take?

	YOUR COUNTRY	ENGLAND	SPAIN
SHOPS open? close?		9 a.m.	8.30 a.m.
WORK start? finish?		5.30 p.m.	10.00 p.m.
SCHOOL start? finish?		8.50 a.m.	1.30 p.m
CINEMAS start? finish?		8.00 p.m.	1.00 a.m.

AMSTERDAM AIRPORT

ARRIVALS (a.m.)	
PARIS	10.30
NEW YORK	9.00
STOCKHOLM	
SÃO PAULO	
LONDON	8.50
HAMBURG	9.10
FARO	
MEXICO CITY	11.15
BERLIN	
FUNCHAL	

DEPARTURES (a.m.)	
MADRID	10.25
LONDON	
LISBON	
WASHINGTON	11.40
RIO DE JANEIRO	9.15
OSLO	
PARIS	
ATHENS	
ROME	10.05
JOHANNESBURG	9.30

How many planes can you see land and take off between
a) 9.00 a.m. – 10.00 a.m?
b) 10.00 a.m. – 11.00 a.m?

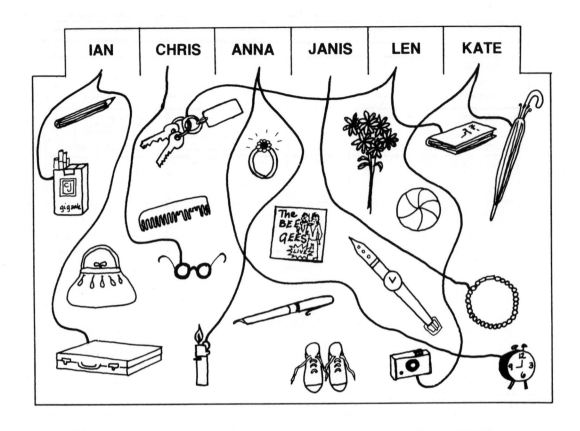

IAN   CHRIS   ANNA   JANIS   LEN   KATE

✓ = stolen
✗ = not stolen

THE JONES

money	
jewellery	
clothes	
record-player	
furniture	

THE BROWNS

TV	✓
paintings	✓
money	✗
leather books	✓
jewellery	✗

RONALD

money	
calculator	
leather jacket	
passport	
cheque book	
camera	

ELIZABETH

gold ring	✓
fur coat	✓
money	✗
watch	✗
radio	✓
antique clock	✗

	Tony TV	Goodbuy TV	Box TV	Tanya TV
How high?		33 cms		40 cms
How wide?		18 cms		20 cms
How long?		41 cms		55 cms
How heavy?		12 kilos		15 kilos
How much?		£170		£190

Which TV will you buy?

SAM:	16 yrs 6' (1.83 m) 9 st (57 kg)
GEORGE:	5' 1" (1.55 m)
JOHN:	15 yrs 9½ st (60 kg)
MARION:	13 yrs 5' 5" (1.65 m)
JUDY:	10½ st (67 kg)
VANESSA:	

Cowboy films	boring exciting interesting _____
Cartoons	fascinating silly hilarious _____
News bulletins	excellent uninteresting all right _____
Quiz programmes	funny dull reasonable _____
Horror films	awful fascinating boring _____

Variety shows	amusing all right terrible _____
Detective films	superb interesting bad _____
Political programmes	uninteresting all right awful _____
Sports programmes	fantastic boring good _____
Documentaries	excellent dull reasonable _____

	Mrs Thomas	Mr Jones	Miss Evans
Matt	Average		
Jane	Very good		
Derek	Weak		Fair
Mike	Lazy		Reasonable
Anne	Fair		
Tony	Hard-working		Good
Teresa	Lazy		Average
Pam	Good		
Mark	Fair		Very good

Final Mark

	Tony	Alison	Ron	Jim and Lyn	Betty
Month?	July			July	
How long?	2 weeks				10 days
Country?		Greece	Spain		France
Town?		Athens	Malaga		Cannes
Travel?	by road			by plane	
Where / stay?		flat	tent	first-class hotel	at her aunt's
Going with?	girlfriend	boyfriend			
Plans?	ride in a gondola eat spaghetti			see the palace walk in the country	

The Island of Primera

Key: Sunbathe ☀ Go waterskiing
       Go fishing   Play golf ✓
       Go diving   Go horseriding
       Go skiing   Go surfing ∿∿

	You	Your friend
1 Where? How long? What/do?		
2 Where? How long? What/do?		
3 Where? How long? What/do?		
4 Where? How long? What/do?		

	May/Might	Probably	Definitely
SUN			
CLOUDS			
RAIN			
WIND			
SNOW			

NORTHERN SCOTLAND

WESTERN SCOTLAND

SOUTHERN SCOTLAND

THE WEST COAST

THE EAST COAST

YORKSHIRE

THE MIDLANDS

WALES

EAST ANGLIA

THE WEST COUNTRY

THE SOUTH EAST

CORNWALL

BEFORE THE YEAR 2000 . . .?

Key: 1 = definite   4 = possible
       2 = almost certain 5 = unlikely
       3 = probable   6 = impossible

	You	Your friend
1. Everyone will speak the same language.		
2. We will be visited by men from outer space.		
3. There will be no more poverty in the world.		
4. We will eat 'food pills' rather than normal food.		
5. An atomic war will happen.		
6. All cars will be electric.		
7. Every family will have a car.		
8. Married couples will be allowed to have only 2 children.		
9. School will be voluntary for children.		
10. Men and women will only work 25 hours a week.		
11. When we telephone someone we will see them on a screen at the same time.		
12. People will go to live on the moon.		

✓ = agrees
✗ = disagrees

	TONY	SUE	THEIR PARENTS		
1. Pupils should stay at school until they are 16.	✓		✓		
2. Pupils should wear school uniforms.	✗	✗			
3. Boys and girls should study in different schools.			✓		
4. Pupils should have homework every evening.	✗	✓			
5. Girls should be taught cookery and boys woodwork.	✗		✓		
6. Pupils should begin English in primary school.			✗		
7. Pupils should pay to go to school.		✓			
8. Pupils should be allowed to smoke at school.			✗		
9. Pupils should have a shorter summer holiday.		✗			
10. Pupils should have exams every term.	✓	✓			

	1	2	3	4	5	6	7	8	9	10
Disagree										
Agree										

The Bees Knees

John

football X	meat X	wine	going to discos
rugby	fish	beer	eating out
tennis	eggs	whisky	listening to music

Dave

wine	going to discos	meat X	football
beer	eating out	fish	rugby
whisky	listening to music X	eggs	tennis

Jack

going to discos	wine X	football	meat
eating out	beer	rugby	fish X
listening to music	whisky	tennis	eggs

Rob

wine	football	meat	going to discos
beer	rugby	fish	eating out X
whisky X	tennis	eggs	listening to music

Sam

meat	going to discos	wine	football
fish	eating out	beer X	rugby X
eggs	listening to music	whisky	tennis

The Bees Knees' favourite

Sport		Drink	
Food		Evening Activity	

		You	
DRINK	Orange Juice		
	Coca-Cola		
	Lemonade		
FOOD	Crisps		
	Cakes		
	Sandwiches		
MUSIC	Rock		
	Pop		
	Folk		

	Jane	Sue	Tom	Jack
Orange Juice				✓
Coca-Cola		✓		
Lemonade				
Crisps				
Cakes			✓	
Sandwiches				✓
Rock				
Pop	✓	✓		
Folk				

Food _____ Drink _____ Music _____

	WORK	HEALTH	MONEY	SOCIAL LIFE
Joanna	work less	relax	save some money	go to more parties
Philip				
Mark	spend longer at work	play more sport	spend less	visit his friends
Amelia				
Susanna	arrive on time	stop smoking	put her money in the bank	watch T.V. less
Robert				

I – YOUR FAMILY HAS DECIDED TO LIVE IN ENGLAND NEXT YEAR. YOU WILL GO TO AN ENGLISH SCHOOL.
You are worried because:
1. You don't speak English very well yet.
2. You don't want to leave your friends.
3. You don't like the English weather.

4. _____

POSSIBLE ADVICE TO GIVE YOUR FRIEND
– try and teach her
– speak slowly
– be very kind to her
– take her out with you
– show her around
– draw her a map

II – YOU HAVE BEEN OFFERED A JOB MAKING A FILM IN THE AMAZON JUNGLE.
You are worried because:
1. You hate hot weather.
2. There may be lots of insects.
3. It may be dangerous.

4. _____

POSSIBLE ADVICE TO GIVE YOUR FRIEND
– learn to swim
– take a life-jacket
– take lots of books
– keep a diary
– write letters
– telephone from each port

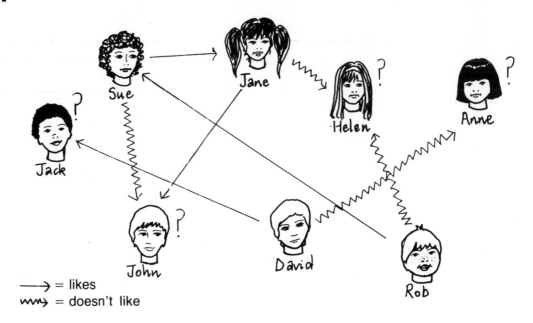

—→ = likes

〜〜〜〜→ = doesn't like

BOB STEVENS
28 years old
Teacher

CHRIS YOUNG
27 years old
Salesman

JEAN DAWSON
25 years old
Secretary

SALLY DAVIS
23 years old
Air hostess

	Chris	Bob	Jean	Sally
Eating out		no	yes	
Listening to music	very much			not at all
Watching TV		yes		not very much
Travelling	no		not at all	
Playing sport	yes	a lot		
Getting up early			not very much	yes
Going for walks	not at all	very much		
Swimming			not at all	very much

Sarah	
Judy	
Nina	fell off her bicycle
Liz	missed the train
Jane	
Jenny	mother's car broke down
Debbie	
Gail	didn't feel well

Max	
Nick	had to go to the Dentist's
James	overslept
Steve	
Phil	missed the bus
Chris	
Nigel	the school bus was late
John	

You are invited to
a party
at Pete's house.
Saturday 8.00 p.m.

John ✗ on holiday ....
Sam and Sue ✗ visiting relations ....
Ian and Tina ✓
Karen ✗ ....
Helen ✗ ....
Jan ✓
Mark and Jean ✗ ....
Linda ✗ ....
Dave ✓
Stan ✗ ....

Caroline ....
George and Mary ....
Pete ....
Sandra ....
Clare ....
Jim and Anna ....
Joanna ....
Julian ....
Ben and Jane ....
Sally ....

24A

	Morning	Afternoon	Evening
Sunday	go to church		go to the concert with Anne
Monday		meet Jane in town	
Tuesday	have my German lesson		
Wednesday		go to the Doctor's	go to the theatre with Joan
Thursday			
Friday	have my driving lesson		
Saturday		go to the hospital	go to a restaurant with Bob

Invite your friend:

Morning:

    meet at a cafe
    go for a walk in the woods

Afternoon:

    listen to records at home
    visit the castle

Evening:

    go out for dinner
    come to my party

	Morning	Afternoon	Evening
Sunday			
Monday	school		
Tuesday	school		
Wednesday	school		
Thursday	school		
Friday	school		
Saturday	school		

This is YOUR

You are going to the Supermarket

GREENGROCER'S

APPLES

PINEAPPLES

CARROTS

CABBAGES

BANANAS

BEANS

PEAS

STRAWBERRIES

Shopping list

bottle of lemonade
packet of crisps
cakes
biscuits
jar of coffee
cheese
jam
sugar

Chez Zé

MENU

Starters:

Main courses:

Vegetables:

Desserts:

Drinks:

POSSIBLE MENU

Starters:
Fish soup
Vegetable soup
Prawn cocktail
Orange juice
Melon
Egg mayonnaise

Main courses:
Fried fish
Roast beef
Roast chicken
Cheese omelette
Chicken and rice
Fish pie

Vegetables:
Chips
Boiled potatoes
Carrots
Beans
Peas
Salad

Desserts:
Apple pie
Ice cream
Strawberries and cream
Chocolate cake
Lemon meringue
Fresh fruit

Drinks:
Beer
Wine
Coca-Cola
Orange juice
Lemonade
Mineral water

THE TRAVEL-THROUGH-TIME POTION

First, put some milk in a bowl.
Then, add some strawberry jam. Stir well.
Next, heat the milk and jam together slowly.
After that, add 1 bar of chocolate. Continue to stir.
Finally, leave the potion to cool.

Drink 2 glasses just before you go to bed.

THE BECOME-INVISIBLE POTION

Drink slowly from pink glasses 6 hours before you travel.

THE PASS-ALL-EXAMS POTION

First, put some sugar in a bowl.
Then, add the juice of 6 lemons and 4 oranges.
Next, add 6 eggs.
After that, leave the mixture in the freezer for 24 hours.
Finally, add fresh cream and nuts.

Eat slowly in small quantities early in the morning.

THE CHANGE-YOUR-IDENTITY ICE CREAM

Drink very cold just before the exam.

Uncle Bill (next Wednesday)
Suggest: a) a box of chocolates
          b) a pen
          c) a hat

Rita (next Monday)
Suggest: a) a bracelet
          b) some flowers
          c) a budgerigar

Joanna (next Friday)
Suggest: a) some perfume
          b) a handbag
          c) a tennis racket

The twins, Sally and Sam
    their record player is broken
    have no time to read
    love seeing plays

Joseph
    doesn't like beer or wine
    only likes pop music
    loves motor-racing

Mary
    already has many plants
    has got three cats
    likes expensive perfume

CHANNEL I

6.00	Improve your English!
6.45	Rock Music Today
7.30	Book Review
8.00	The News
8.20	Star Blaze: *space film*
9.00	The Pink Panther: *cartoon*
9.30	Miss World
10.30	Epilogue

CHANNEL II

6.00	Athletics
6.45	Tom and Jerry: *cartoons*
7.30	Eugénia: *Brazilian serial*
8.00	Parlez-vous Français?
8.20	Eurovision Song Contest – Part I
9.00	The News
9.30	Eurovision Song Contest – Part II
10.30	Bed-time Story

CHANNEL III

6.00	The News
6.45	Car Rally
7.30	Inside Africa: *documentary*
8.00	Win a Fortune: *quiz*
8.20	Murder on the Beach: *spy film*
9.00	Symphony Concert
9.30	Football
10.30	Poem for Today

TIME	You	Your Friend	Final Choice
6.00			
6.45			
7.30			
8.00			

TIME	You	Your Friend	Final Choice
8.20			
9.00			
9.30			
10.30			

DINOSAURS

Dinosaur is the name of a group of extinct reptiles. The name comes from Latin and means 'terrible lizard'. Some dino- saurs were enormous. The big- gest were 24 m long and weighed 20 tons. Others were quite small. Dinosaurs were only found in Europe and North America. They had enormous heads, long tails and huge bodies. They never ate meat and lived mostly on the land. Some dino- saurs could also swim.

QUEEN VICTORIA

Queen Victoria is one of the most famous characters in English history. She was born in 1825 and had a very happy childhood. She became Queen when she was 15 years old. In 1876 she was also made Empress of India. Victoria married her cousin, Prince Albert in August 1840. They had nine children. Albert and Victoria loved each other very much, and so Victoria was very sad when her husband died in 1860. She lived until 1901 and had 27 grandchildren at the time of her death.

Some facts about **Penguins:**

– live at sea except when they have a family
– mother penguin lays 2 eggs
– Emperor Penguin: over a metre tall
– black and white feathers
– yellow spots on its head

Some facts about **King Charles I:**

– became King of England in 1625
– Civil War began in 1642
– nearly killed in Oxford
– finally defeated in August 1648
– executed January 30th 1649

	MURDERED?	MUGGED?	ROBBED?	STOLEN?
REDBRIDGE	Men: Women: 1 Children:	Men: 10 Women: Children: 17	Houses: Shops: Banks: 4	Cars: 472 Lorries: Bicycles: 503
WHITECHURCH	Children: 1 Men: 1 Women:	Children: 19 Men: Women:	Banks: 2 Houses: 110 Shops:	Bicycles: Cars: Lorries: 27

Which town had more crimes?

THE LANCET TRIBE

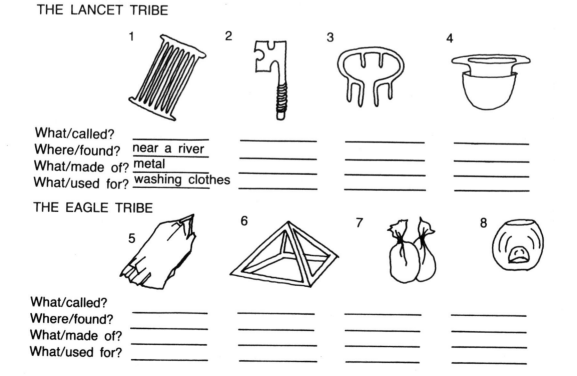

	1	2	3	4
What/called?				
Where/found?	near a river			
What/made of?	metal			
What/used for?	washing clothes			

THE EAGLE TRIBE

5   6   7   8

What/called?
Where/found?
What/made of?
What/used for?

1 2 3 4

Name			Anne Carter	Henry Black
Age			14	13
Country			Canada	Australia

1 2 3 4

Name	Sue Turner		Linda Williams	
Age		32	25	29
Job	Teacher	Postman		
Country			Scotland	

	MARTA	ROB	BEN	PATRICK
shape?		oblong	square	
colour?	white		black and white	
size?		not very big		very large
other information?	doesn't lock			striped

Who will claim which suitcase?

	SAM	PAUL	BARBARA
how many?		1	
shape?	round		
colour?	pale purple		dark green
how big?		enormous	
made of?		glass	metal
other information?	flashing lights		yellow windows

	height	build	hair	eyes	features
NICK REEK	tall			brown	enormous feet
ROBBIE FAST		thin	red curly		
ANNIE ADDER		slim		blue	always wears sunglasses
LORNA STEELE	very tall		long dark		
JAKE JAWS		fat		black	
CHRIS RIPPER	short		brown curly		wears diamond ear-rings

Which three people must you meet?

Tell your friend to meet:

Susan: tall
slim
short dark hair
glasses
wearing: skirt and striped
jacket
carrying: suitcase and
umbrella

John: not very tall
short fair hair
beard
wearing: suit and tie
carrying: briefcase

Jean: short
fat
long fair hair
wearing: shirt and trousers
carrying: jacket and handbag

Arrange on your diagram:

1 sofo

2 armchairs

1 TV table and TV

1 phone table
and phone

1 fireplace

1 bookcase

2 indoor plants

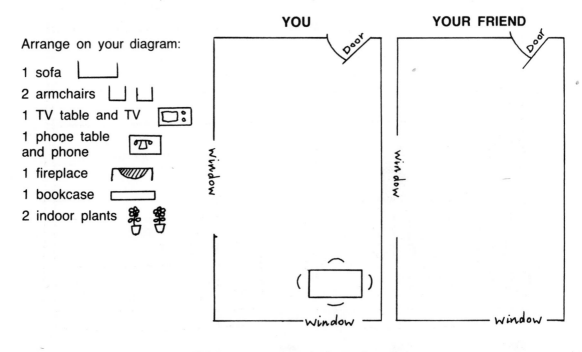

Which arrangement is better?

HELEN	studying at Mike's house
STEVE	having dinner at home with Pam
JOY	visiting her friend, Jenny
ROBIN	having a drink in the pub with Harry
DAN	having dinner in a restaurant with his girlfriend
SHEILA	watching a film on T.V. alone

PAM	
MIKE	
JANE	
JENNY	
GEORGE	
HARRY	

Who was the murderer?

	GETS UP	BREAKFAST	WORK	LUNCH	DINNER	EVENING
TOM JONES BUS DRIVER						
JOHN SMITH BANK MANAGER	8.15	8.30	9.00 – 5.00	1.00 in the office	about 8.00	reads, watches T.V.
SALLY WEST SECRETARY						
JANE NOLES JOURNALIST	7.30	8.15	8.45 – 7.00	1.30 at home	after work	works, goes to the theatre

Time of meeting:

	GETS UP	BREAKFAST	WORK	LUNCH	DINNER	EVENING
BILL TAYLOR SHOPKEEPER						
SUE EVANS WAITRESS						
JEAN SCOTT						
TONY BENSON						

Time of meeting:

	BATH	SYDNEY	NEW ORLEANS	DUNDEE
country?		Australia		Scotland
which part?		the east coast	the south-east	
population?	85,000		600,000	
weather?	mild and rainy		hot and dry	
what/like?	quiet attractive			very old traditional
famous for?		the opera house		cakes

What the TRAVEL AGENT says:

BRECCLES
high in the mountains
mild in the summer
peaceful
good restaurants
beautiful countryside

HELTON
near sandy beaches
many cheap hotels
hot and dry
very few tourists
lots of bars and discos

SEAGATE
uncrowded beaches
good hotels
lots of cheap restaurants
full of young people
long hot summer

What YOU say:

FLIMTON-ON-SEA
dirty beaches
very hot, never rains
noisy
reasonable prices
no cinema, only two cafés

TANAWAY
2 kilometres from lakes
rains a lot
quiet
cheap places to stay
no buses and trains

SLACTON
stony beaches
good weather in summer
lots to do in the evening
many old people
bad, expensive hotels

Which place will you choose?

Ask your partner how to get to:

   a) the Dentist's from Sutton-on-Sea   (Write A in the box)
   b) the Chemist's from Ketton   (Write B in the box)
   c) the Snack Bar from Filby   (Write C in the box)

FENLEY-ON-MEAD

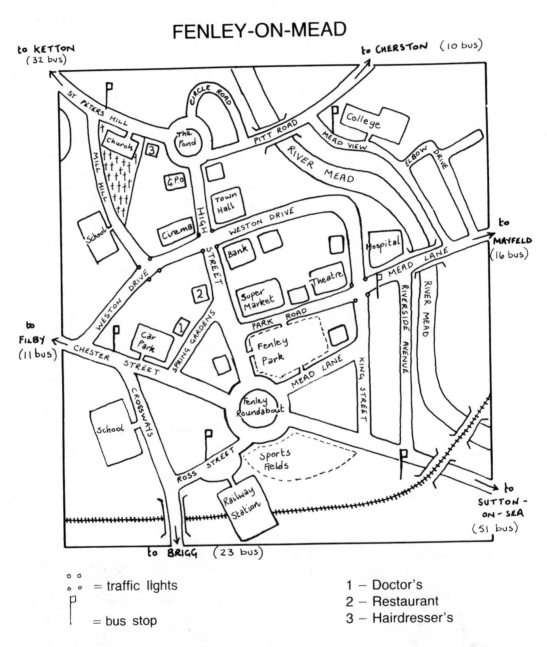

= traffic lights

= bus stop

1 – Doctor's
2 – Restaurant
3 – Hairdresser's

Describe your proposed Carnival Route to your partner.
Which is the better route?

THE EARLIEST ROUND-THE-WORLD EXPLORERS

Name	Started journey		Visited		Adventures	Returned home
	Year	Town	Place	Year		
Jean le Monde French			South Africa	1416	fought alligators	
			India	1417		
John O'World Irish	1420	Dublin	Brazil			1425
			South Africa			
Jan Wereld Dutch	1430	Amsterdam				died of malaria in Brazil (1435)
João Mundo Portuguese			Brazil		found gold in Rio de Janeiro	
			India			

1. Which country is larger?
   a) Portugal
   b) Ireland

   Ireland: 84,000 square kilometres

2. Which of these cities has the oldest
   university?
   a) Lisbon
   b) Lima
   c) Cambridge
   d) Cologne

   Cambridge: started in 1200
   Lisbon: started in 1290

3. Which of these mountains are the
   highest?
   a) The Andes
   b) The Rocky Mountains
   c) The Atlas Mountains

   The Atlas Mountains: 4000 metres
   The Rocky Mountains: 4500 metres

4. Which river is longer?
   a) The Amazon
   b) The Nile

   The Nile: 7000 kilometres

5. Which of these countries has the
   largest population?
   a) France
   b) Spain
   c) West Germany
   d) England

   Spain: 36 million
   England: 46 million

6. Which city is further from London?
   a) Lisbon
   b) Rome

   Lisbon: 1600 kilometres

7. Which ocean is the biggest?
   a) The Atlantic
   b) The Pacific
   c) The Indian

   The Atlantic: 82 million square kilometres
   The Indian: 73 million square kilometres

8. Which of these U.S. cities is the
   largest?
   a) Chicago
   b) Los Angeles
   c) San Francisco

   Chicago: $3\frac{1}{2}$ million
   Los Angeles: 3 million

9. Which town is hotter in summer?
   a) Madrid
   b) Athens

   Madrid: 25°C

10. Which planet is bigger?
    a) The Earth
    b) The Moon

    The Earth: diameter of 12,800 kilometres

THE CORNER CAFE	SKIMPY SNACK BAR

THE CORNER CAFE

Drinks:
Cup of tea (with milk) .... 14 p
Cup of tea (with lemon) ..... 12 p
Glass of milk .... 15 p
Cup of white coffee .... 22 p
Cup of black coffee .... 20 p
Pepsi-Cola .... 20 p
Lemonade .... 17 p

Sandwiches:
Cheese and tomato .... 34 p
Cheese .... 27 p
Ham .... 27 p

Chocolate cake .... 20 p
Lemon pie .... 18 p

SKIMPY SNACK BAR

Drinks:
Cup of black coffee ....
Cup of white coffee ....
Cup of tea (with milk) ....
Glass of milk ....
Coca-Cola ....
Orangeade ....

Sandwiches:
Ham ....
Ham and cheese ....
Cheese and tomato ....
Cheese.........................

Lemon pie......................
Apple tart ....

Which cafe is cheaper?

FROM LONDON TO:	BY BUS	BY TRAIN	BY PLANE
MADRID	£30	£42·50	1 hour 45 minutes
PARIS	11 hours	8 hours	£54
ROME	31 hours £42·50	£60	2 hours
ATHENS	£39	£52	3 hours
LISBON	36 hours	35 hours	£120
BONN		£28-50	50 minutes

LONDON TO LISBON	TRAIN I	TRAIN II	TRAIN III
leave from? time?	14.40 Monday		Victoria station 8.15 Friday
English Channel? how long?	by boat		by boat 3 hours
arrive/ Paris? leave/Paris?	2.05 Tuesday		19.30 Friday 5.45 Saturday
route? arrive/Lisbon?	4.45 Wednesday		Madrid 03.30 Sunday
price: 1st class? price: 2nd class?	£32·50		£46-95 £26-95
restaurant car?			Yes
bar?	1st class only		No
couchettes?	No		No

Which train will you and your friend take?

	YOUR COUNTRY	ENGLAND	SPAIN
SHOPS open? close?		5.00 p.m.	8.00 p.m.
WORK start? finish?		9.30 a.m.	8.00 a.m.
SCHOOL start? finish?		4.30 p.m	8.30 a.m
CINEMAS start? finish?		10.30 p.m.	10.30 p.m

AMSTERDAM AIRPORT

ARRIVALS (a.m.)	
PARIS	
NEW YORK	
STOCKHOLM	11.10
SÃO PAULO	10.30
LONDON	
HAMBURG	
FARO	8.30
MEXICO CITY	
BERLIN	9.45
FUNCHAL	10.50

DEPARTURES (a.m.)	
MADRID	
LONDON	9.40
LISBON	9.05
WASHINGTON	
RIO DE JANEIRO	
OSLO	10.35
PARIS	11.30
ATHENS	11.15
ROME	
JOHANNESBURG	

How many planes can you see land and take off between
a)   9.00 a.m. − 10.00 a.m?
b)   10.00 a.m. − 11.00 a.m?

14B

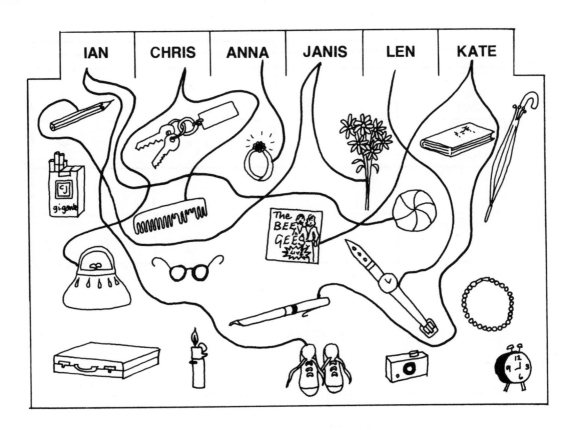

IAN   CHRIS   ANNA   JANIS   LEN   KATE

✓ = stolen
✗ = not stolen

THE BROWNS

money	
jewellery	
paintings	
leather books	
TV	

THE JONES

furniture	✓
clothes	✗
money	✓
jewellery	✓
record-player	✗

ELIZABETH

watch	
gold ring	
radio	
antique clock	
money	
fur coat	

RONALD

camera	✓
cheque book	✗
calculator	✓
money	✗
leather jacket	✗
passport	✓

	Tanya TV	Box TV	Goodbuy TV	Tony TV
How high?		35 cms		25 cms
How wide?		17 cms		15 cms
How long?		40 cms		30 cms
How heavy?		18 kilos		10 kilos
How much?		£200		£130

Which TV will you buy?

VANESSA:	14 yrs 4'10" (1.47 m) 6½ st (41 kg)
MARION:	7½ st (48 kg)
JUDY:	15 yrs 5'9" (1.75 m)
GEORGE:	14 yrs 10 st (64 kg)
JOHN:	5'7" (1.70 m)
SAM:	

Cowboy films	boring exciting interesting _____
Cartoons	fascinating silly hilarious _____
News bulletins	excellent uninteresting all right _____
Quiz programmes	funny dull reasonable _____
Horror films	awful fascinating boring _____

Variety shows	amusing all right terrible _____
Detective films	superb interesting bad _____
Political programmes	uninteresting all right awful _____
Sports programmes	fantastic boring good _____
Documentaries	excellent dull reasonable _____

	Mr Jones	Mrs Thomas	Miss Evans
Teresa	Weak		
Pam	Lazy		Fair
Matt	Excellent		Reasonable
Mark	Average		
Mike	Good		
Jane	Good		Hard-working
Derek	Fair		
Tony	Excellent		
Anne	Weak		Good

Final Mark

	Tony	Alison	Ron	Jim and Lyn	Betty
Month?		August	September		August
How long?		3 weeks	2 weeks	2 weeks	
Country?	Italy			Portugal	
Town?	Venice			Sintra	
Travel?		by plane	by train		by car
Where / stay?	cheap hotel				
Going with?			alone	two children	her dog
Plans?		lie on the beach go to discos	lie on the beach visit Grenada		go to the film festival visit Monte Carlo

The Island of Primera

UPTOWN
PLATT TOWN
RIVERLY
ROSATOWN
WEST POINT
REDHILL
EAST BAY
CLIFFTOWN
HIGHTOWN

Key: Sunbathe ※   Go waterskiing
      Go fishing   Play golf ✓
      Go diving   Go horseriding
      Go skiing   Go surfing ∼

	You	Your friend
1 Where? How long? What/do?		
2 Where? How long? What/do?		
3 Where? How long? What/do?		
4 Where? How long? What/do?		

	May/might	Probably	Definitely
SUN			
CLOUDS			
RAIN			
WIND			
SNOW			

NORTHERN SCOTLAND

WESTERN SCOTLAND

SOUTHERN SCOTLAND

THE WEST COAST

THE EAST COAST

YORKSHIRE

THE MIDLANDS

WALES

EAST ANGLIA

THE WEST COUNTRY

THE SOUTH EAST

CORNWALL

BEFORE THE YEAR 2000 . . . ?

Key: 1 = definite   4 = possible
      2 = almost certain   5 = unlikely
      3 = probable   6 = impossible

	You	Your friend

1. Everyone will speak the same language.
2. We will be visited by men from outer space.
3. There will be no more poverty in the world.
4. We will eat 'food pills' rather than normal food.
5. An atomic war will happen.
6. All cars will be electric.
7. Every family will have a car.
8. Married couples will be allowed to have only 2 children.
9. School will be voluntary for children.
10. Men and women will only work 25 hours a week.
11. When we telephone someone we will see them on a screen at the same time.
12. People will go to live on the moon.

✓ = agrees
✗ = disagrees

	TONY	SUE	THEIR PARENTS		
1. Pupils should stay at school until they are 16.		✓			
2. Pupils should wear school uniforms.			✓		
3. Boys and girls should study in different schools.	✗	✓			
4. Pupils should have homework every evening.			✗		
5. Girls should be taught cookery and boys woodwork.		✗			
6. Pupils should begin English in primary school.	✓	✓			
7. Pupils should pay to go to school.	✗		✗		
8. Pupils should be allowed to smoke at school.	✗	✗			
9. Pupils should have a shorter summer holiday.	✓		✓		
10. Pupils should have exams every term.			✓		

	1	2	3	4	5	6	7	8	9	10
Disagree										
Agree										

The Bees Knees

John	football / rugby / tennis	meat / fish / eggs	wine X / beer / whisky	going to discos / eating out / listening to music X
Dave	wine X / beer / whisky	going to discos / eating out / listening to music	meat / fish / eggs	football / rugby / tennis X
Jack	going to discos X / eating out / listening to music	wine / beer / whisky	football X / rugby / tennis	meat / fish / eggs
Rob	wine / beer / whisky	football X / rugby / tennis	meat X / fish / eggs	going to discos / eating out / listening to music
Sam	meat / fish X / eggs	going to discos / eating out X / listening to music	wine / beer / whisky	football / rugby / tennis

The Bees Knees' favourite

Sport		Drink	
Food		Evening Activity	

		You	
DRINK	Orange Juice		
	Coca-Cola		
	Lemonade		
FOOD	Crisps		
	Cakes		
	Sandwiches		
MUSIC	Rock		
	Pop		
	Folk		

	Jane	Sue	Tom	Jack
Orange Juice				
Coca-Cola	✓			
Lemonade			✓	
Crisps		✓		
Cakes				
Sandwiches	✓			
Rock				✓
Pop				
Folk			✓	

Food _____ Drink _____ Music _____

	WORK	HEALTH	MONEY	SOCIAL LIFE
Joanna				
Philip	work harder	go for more walks	stop worrying about money	meet more people
Mark				
Amelia	find a new job	eat less	spend more on herself	make new friends
Susanna				
Robert	leave work earlier	drink less	be more generous	spend more time at home

I – YOUR FAMILY HAS INVITED YOUR FRENCH COUSIN TO COME AND LIVE WITH YOU.

You are worried because:
1. She doesn't speak your language.
2. She may feel homesick.
3. She doesn't know your town.

4. _____

POSSIBLE ADVICE TO GIVE YOUR FRIEND
– work harder at English
– make an English pen-friend
– write letters
– invite friends for holidays
– take warm clothes
– take an umbrella

II – YOU ARE GOING TO SAIL ROUND THE WORLD WITH YOUR RICH UNCLE.

You are worried because:
1. You can't swim.
2. It may be a very long journey.
3. Your parents think it may be dangerous.

4. _____

POSSIBLE ADVICE TO GIVE YOUR FRIEND
– take cool clothes
– stay in the shade
– take insect cream
– sleep in a tent
– always be careful
– make friends with local people

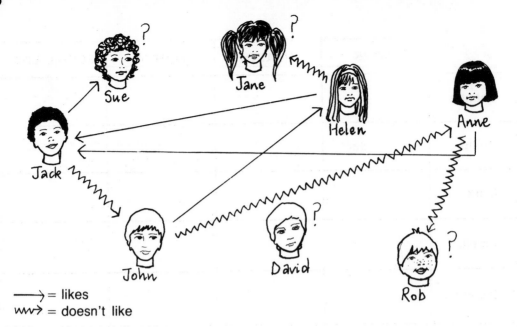

→ = likes
ww→ = doesn't like

BOB STEVENS
28 years old
Teacher

CHRIS YOUNG
27 years old
Salesman

JEAN DAWSON
25 years old
Secretary

SALLY DAVIS
23 years old
Air hostess

	Chris	Bob	Jean	Sally
Eating out	yes			no
Listening to music		a lot	yes	
Watching TV	not at all		very much	
Travelling		yes		very much
Playing sport			no	not very much
Getting up early	no	not very much		
Going for walks			yes	no
Swimming	a lot	no		

Sarah	missed the bus
Judy	overslept
Nina	
Liz	
Jane	had to go to the Doctor's
Jenny	
Debbie	her watch was slow
Gail	

Max	forgot his books
Nick	
James	
Steve	father's car had no petrol
Phil	
Chris	alarm clock didn't ring
Nigel	
John	missed the train

> You are invited to
> a party
> at Pete's house.
> Saturday 8.00 p.m.

Caroline ✗ studying for her exams ....
George and Mary ✗ their son is ill ......
Pete ✓
Sandra ✗ ....
Clare ✓
Jim and Anna ✗ ....
Joanna ✓
Julian ✗ ....
Ben and Jane ✗ ....
Sally ✗ ....

John ....
Sam and Sue ....
Ian and Tina ....
Karen ....
Helen ....
Jan ....
Mark and Jean ....
Linda ....
Dave ....
Stan ....

	Morning	Afternoon	Evening
Sunday		drive to the sea-side	
Monday	go to the Dentist's		
Tuesday			go to the cinema with Carol
Wednesday		have tea with Anne	
Thursday	have my hair cut		have dinner with Tony
Friday	have my French lesson	go horse-riding with Bob	
Saturday			go to John's party

Invite your friend:

Morning:

go for a walk on the beach
play tennis

Afternoon:

go to the swimming pool
go to the park

Evening:

have dinner at home
see a film

	Morning	Afternoon	Evening
Sunday			
Monday	school		
Tuesday	school		
Wednesday	school		
Thursday	school		
Friday	school		
Saturday	school		

This is YOUR

You are going to the Greengrocer's

SUPERMARKET

LEMONADE

CHEESE

SUGAR

COFFEE

MILK

CORNFLAKES

ICE CREAM

Shopping list

6 bananas
5 kilos of potatoes
1 kilo of oranges
2 kilos of apples
a cabbage
a pineapple
1 kilo of onions
4 pears

Chez Zé

MENU

Starters:

Main courses:

Vegetables:

Desserts:

Drinks:

POSSIBLE MENU

Starters:
Fish soup
Vegetable soup
Prawn cocktail
Orange juice
Melon
Egg mayonnaise

Main courses:
Fried fish
Roast beef
Roast chicken
Cheese omelette
Chicken and rice
Fish pie

Vegetables:
Chips
Boiled potatoes
Carrots
Beans
Peas
Salad

Desserts:
Apple pie
Ice cream
Strawberries and cream
Chocolate cake
Lemon meringue
Fresh fruit

Drinks:
Beer
Wine
Coca-Cola
Orange juice
Lemonade
Mineral water

THE BECOME-INVISIBLE POTION

First, put 2 eggs in a bowl.
Then, add the juice of 1 orange and 3 strawberries.
Next, mix in half a cup of milk.
After that, add some sugar and the petals of a wild flower.
Finally, add 3 drops of sweet port wine.

Drink slowly from pink glasses 6 hours before you travel.

THE TRAVEL-THROUGH-TIME POTION

Drink 2 glasses just before you go to bed.

THE CHANGE-YOUR-IDENTITY ICE CREAM

First, cut up 4 bananas and put them in a bowl.
Then, add some honey.
Next, pour boiling water onto the bananas and leave them for 3 hours.
After that, pour in a cup of fresh cream. Stir well.
Finally, add some ice.

Drink very cold just before the exam.

THE PASS-ALL-EXAMS POTION

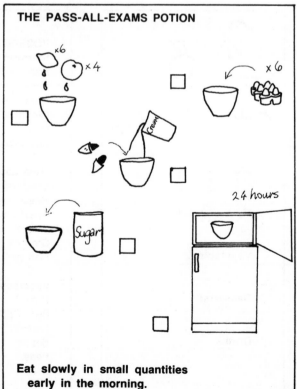

Eat slowly in small quantities early in the morning.

The twins, Sally and Sam (next Sunday)
Suggest: a) a record
          b) a book
          c) two theatre tickets

Joseph (next Thursday)
Suggest: a) a bottle of wine
          b) a tape of classical music
          c) a book on cars

Mary (next Tuesday)
Suggest: a) an indoor plant
          b) a puppy
          c) some French perfume

Uncle Bill
    doesn't like sweets
    got a pen for Christmas
    has just lost his favourite hat

Rita
    never wears jewellery
    has a lovely garden, full of flowers
    loves all types of pets

Joanna
    doesn't like cosmetics
    is going to receive a handbag from Tom
    broke her racket last week

CHANNEL I

6.00	Improve your English!
6.45	Rock Music Today
7.30	Book Review
8.00	The News
8.20	Star Blaze: *space film*
9.00	The Pink Panther: *cartoon*
9.30	Miss World
10.30	Epilogue

CHANNEL II

6.00	Athletics
6.45	Tom and Jerry: *cartoons*
7.30	Eugénia: *Brazilian serial*
8.00	Parlez-vous Français?
8.20	Eurovision Song Contest – Part I
9.00	The News
9.30	Eurovision Song Contest – Part II
10.30	Bed-time Story

CHANNEL III

6.00	The News
6.45	Car Rally
7.30	Inside Africa: *documentary*
8.00	Win a Fortune: *quiz*
8.20	Murder on the Beach: *spy film*
9.00	Symphony Concert
9.30	Football
10.30	Poem for Today

TIME	You	Your Friend	Final Choice
6.00			
6.45			
7.30			
8.00			

TIME	You	Your Friend	Final Choice
8.20			
9.00			
9.30			
10.30			

PENGUINS

Penguins are found on cold, rocky coasts all over the world. They live most of their lives on land and make their nests low on the ground. The mother penguin lays 6 eggs. Both mother and father penguin look after the baby penguins when they are born. The largest penguin in the world is the Emperor Penguin which is nearly half a metre tall. It lives near the South Pole. Its feathers are black and grey and it has orange spots on its head.

KING CHARLES I

Charles I was the son of James VI of Scotland and Anne of Denmark. He was born in 1590 and became King of England in 1620. Charles disagreed with many Englishmen and in 1643 a Civil War began. At first his army did well, but in 1646, Charles was nearly killed in Cambridge. He escaped from the city but he was finally defeated in July 1648. He spent the next few months in the Tower of London and on January 1st 1649 he was executed.

Some facts about **Dinosaurs:**

— dinosaur, Greek name
— biggest dinosaur weighed 39 tons
— dinosaurs found in China and South Africa
— dinosaurs had small heads
— some dinosaurs ate meat

Some facts about **Queen Victoria:**

— born in 1819
— became Queen when she was 18 years old
— married Prince Albert in February 1840
— Prince Albert died in 1861
— Victoria had 37 grandchildren when she died

	MURDERED?	MUGGED?	ROBBED?	STOLEN?
REDBRIDGE	Men: 1 Women: Children: 2	Men: Women: 23 Children:	Houses: 135 Shops: 25 Banks:	Cars: Lorries: 38 Bicycles:
WHITECHURCH	Men: Women: 2 Children:	Men: Women: 27 Children:	Houses: Shops: 30 Banks:	Cars: 391 Lorries: Bicycles: 421

Which town had more crimes?

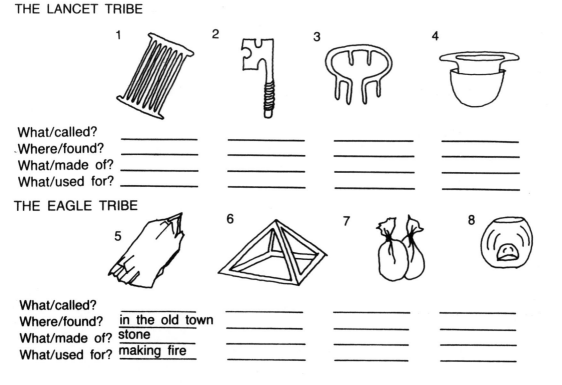

THE LANCET TRIBE

1   2   3   4

What/called? _____ _____ _____ _____
Where/found? _____ _____ _____ _____
What/made of? _____ _____ _____ _____
What/used for? _____ _____ _____ _____

THE EAGLE TRIBE

5   6   7   8

What/called? _____ _____ _____ _____
Where/found? in the old town _____ _____ _____
What/made of? stone _____ _____ _____
What/used for? making fire _____ _____ _____